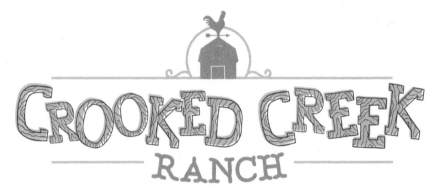

CROOKED CREEK
RANCH

By
Amy Drorbaugh

Illustrated by
Victoria Skakandi

CONTENTS

CHAPTER ONE

THE TOMATO BATH

"Shhhh, you're going to scare her away!"

Three little blonde heads peeked over the fallen tree; six little grubby hands rested on the rough bark of the old oak. Tommy motioned for his brother and sister to stay down. At ten years old, he was the designated leader of the group and technically in charge of the younger kids. Every time they left the ranch house to play in the California hills surrounding their cattle ranch, Ma would call out, "Keep an eye on the littles!" And he tried his best, but everyone knew it was tiny six-year-old Sara, with her wild curls and dancing eyes, who was the real boss. The two brothers adored their little sister because she always came up with the best ideas for playing. In fact, she was the reason they were all hiding behind the old dead tree.

The three Smith children had all been sitting on the bank of the creek that ran through their back pasture and gave their ranch its name—Crooked Creek Ranch. The stream wound its way back and forth across their entire spread. During the spring the creek would swell with snow runoff and race through the meadow, but now in early fall, it was reduced to a slow trickle, only two feet across. Tommy had been making little boats out of sticks and leaves and sailing them in the slow water. Eight-year-old Levi had been digging a hole in the bank as it slowly filled up with cold muddy water, while Sara lazily watched the cows grazing in the lower pasture. Looking up, Tommy noticed the sun had started to dip into the tree line on the mountain that formed the western half of the canyon they called home. He was thinking it was time to start back when Sara suddenly yelled out, "Look! Look over there!"

Sara pointed downstream toward the dirt road that snaked around trees and boulders and led out of their canyon. Tommy and Levi stood up to see what she was so excited about. They both gasped when they saw where she was pointing.

There she was, under the old oak tree with the low branches that brushed the ground—a big mama skunk. And right behind her, in a line, were three roly-poly, fluffy little skunk babies.

"Aren't they so cute!" squealed Sara, clapping her hands together. "Let's catch them!"

"Catch them?" Tommy frowned. He looked again at the setting sun. It would be dark soon, and Ma would be looking for them to come home.

"Yes! There are three of them and three of us; we could each keep one for our own special pet." Without waiting for either reply or agreement, Sara crouched down and started sneaking toward the mama skunk. "C'mon, and keep quiet."

Levi, always ready to follow Sara into fun—adventure or trouble—immediately bent over and followed his little sister. Tommy hesitated, looking again at the reddish sky. He knew from experience that getting Sara to change her mind would be hard, and the idea of a small soft baby skunk for his very own was too exciting to resist.

He shrugged his shoulders and crept quickly after the others toward the fallen tree. The old dead tree had been leaning all year long and had finally fallen over during the last big storm. Soon, Pa and the uncles would come out with their axes and saws and cut it up to use for firewood over the cold winter, but for now it made the perfect hiding spot for three small children.

Tommy peered over the log to judge how far away the skunks were. Unaware of the fate being planned for them, the four black-and-white animals were snuffling around the base of the tree, looking for earthworms or berries to eat. If things worked out, they might even find a lizard. Skunks love lizards.

Tommy sank back down behind the log and took charge. "Here's what we'll do: Sara, you go down around that end of the log, and Levi, you sneak the other way. We need to get as close as we can before they see us. Once we are super close, we can each grab one and then run before the mama skunk sprays us."

Sara nodded, her tongue caught between her teeth as she concentrated on the baby skunk she wanted. Levi peered over the log and blurted out, "I want the one with the big, bushy tail!"

But he spoke too loudly. The mother skunk looked up, alert to the sudden danger. She let out a funny squeal and started herding her babies toward the protection of a pile of boulders. She could move surprisingly fast.

"They're getting away!" Sara howled and charged around the end of the log. "Get 'em!" Levi was right on her heels, whooping a battle cry.

Helplessly, Tommy watched as Levi and Sara

both ran after the fleeing skunks. The mama skunk, seeing the two children coming, hissed angrily and dashed for the rocks. Reaching the pile, she shoved her babies into a small gap between two large rocks, pushing them in with her nose. She turned around, and right as the children came within range, she raised her tail, aimed, and fired her most effective weapon.

Levi, who was in front, took the brunt of the first spray, but Tommy and Sara, catching up, got well covered by the second spray. All three children started coughing and gagging as the stench filled the air around them, sticking to their clothes, skin, and hair. Sara was the first to recover, brushing aside the incident and focusing on the prize. She wanted that skunk baby.

"C'mon, she already sprayed us; let's grab the babies and run."

But Tommy had had enough. He knew that mama skunks could spray five or six times before they were done. He could also see that there was no way to get to the baby skunks underneath the big rock without getting the mother skunk to come out.

"No, Sara, it's time to go home. 'Sides, those baby skunks probably need their mama. They wouldn't be happy with us with no forest or earthworms or nothin'." As he spoke, Tommy grabbed his siblings' hands and started towing them back toward the creek. Sara looked over her shoulder longingly one last time, but she allowed Tommy to pull her along.

The children jumped the creek and scampered up the gentle hill, weaving through the gnarled oak trees and pushing through the brush. Once they reached the top, they could see the ranch house, with a welcoming curl of smoke rising from the chimney.

They were later than normal; Ma was on the wide front porch waiting for them. She raised her hand when they appeared, and they broke into a trot to reach her faster.

"It's suppertime; where have you been?" Ma was a tall, strong woman, and her broad, sun-browned face wrinkled up as she grinned. But as the children got closer, the smile slid right off her face. "By thunder! What happened to y'all? You smell worse than your father's riding boots. No, no, don't talk, and don't come any closer. Go right around the house to the horse trough and take off those clothes. I'll meet you there." Ma went back inside with a swish of skirts and a bang of the screen door.

The children exchanged sheepish looks and

headed to the back of the ranch house. Behind the house itself was the large barn where the horses, milk cow, dogs, cats, one fat pig, and chickens slept. There was also a corral for the horses during the daytime and several large round metal troughs for the animals to drink from.

Sara untied her apron and pulled off her overdress. "Why do you think Ma wanted us to come back here?" she asked as she put the dress aside.

"She doesn't want us stinkin' up the house, I guess." Tommy's voice was muffled from inside his shirt as he pulled it off.

"Aww," protested Levi, "I don't think we smell that bad. I reckon that skunk mostly missed us, anyhow."

"You reckon wrong, mister," Ma corrected,

emerging from the back of the ranch house. "You stink to high heaven." She was carrying a basket full of bright red tomatoes and a bar of lye soap, and she had pinched a clothespin onto the end of her nose. "Now, into the trough with you all."

Levi whooped with delight and jumped into the nearest trough, half-full with water from their spring, Tommy right behind him. Sara, however, looked at the dark water, covered with floating hay and twigs and grass, and moss and slime growing up the sides, and she wrinkled her nose. "But it's so dirty!" she protested, her lower lip jutting out.

"No arguing, little miss," Ma said firmly, but with a twinkle in her eye. "Little girls who play with skunks can't be picky."

Sara reluctantly climbed over the side of the trough, her feet sliding a little on the slimy

bottom. She tried not to complain about the
cold water or the mild burn of the lye soap as
her mother scrubbed her down, since the whole
thing had been her idea in the first place. She
was grateful when Ma finally let them rinse
off and climb out of the trough. Grabbing her
clothes, she headed for the house.

"Hang on there, Sara-Bear," Ma called out.
"We're not done yet."

And with that Ma picked up a red, juicy
tomato and squashed it down on top of Sara's
blonde curls.

"Hey!" Sara squealed as the juices ran down
the side of her face and into her ear. Tommy
and Levi busted up laughing at the shocked
expression on their sister's face.

"You, too, boys. Come grab some tomatoes and
start rubbing them all over. It's the best way to

get rid of the smell." She took another tomato and crushed it in her hands and started rubbing it up and down Sara's arms. The boys jumped for the basket and immediately started bursting tomatoes and smearing them everywhere. They were a funny sight, standing there in their underwear, soaking wet, and covered in tomato juice. Then back into the trough they went for one more rinse.

Even then, Ma wouldn't let them back into the house. She shooed them into the barn, where they found seats on the saddle blankets, and she carried their reeking clothes away on a pitchfork. She was back in minutes with their dinner and nightclothes. As they gulped down the stew and gobbled up the corn bread, sticky with honey, Ma made up a bed for them in the hayloft.

"You can't sleep inside tonight. The tomatoes

got a lot of the smell off, but some of it will just have to wear off naturally," explained Ma. "We don't want to stink up the house."

Tommy grinned around a mouthful of corn bread. "You mean we get to sleep out here tonight?" He smiled at Levi in anticipation—a whole night outside!

Ma smiled. "That's right. Now finish that up and crawl into your blankets. I've got mending yet to do tonight." With a kiss she tucked each child into their deep hay bed and tried not to grimace too much at the smell. She said good night as she gathered up the dinner plates and headed back into the house.

Warm and tired in her blankets, Sara sleepily called out, "I never want to see another skunk for the rest of my whole life!"

"What are you talking about?" Levi yawned.

"This was the best day ever! We got to go swimming, eat in the barn, and now we get to sleep outside." Tommy murmured his agreement, already half asleep with their dog, Flash, sprawled across his stomach. Sara shook her head. Nothing was worth having to take a tomato bath—not even a roly-poly skunk baby!

CHAPTER TWO

THE BEAR AND THE SOAP

Uncle Reuben pushed back from the table with a loud belch. "Jo, that was the best sweet potato pie on this side of the Rockies."

Sara waited for her ma to scold Uncle for his bad manners, but she just laughed and dropped another slice of pie on his plate. Uncle Reuben was the only one who called Ma "Jo" instead of her full name of Joanne or Ma Smith.

A giant of a man with a round, jolly face almost completely covered in a bushy black beard, there was something about Reuben Smith that just made you smile. Everything about him was loud, from his booming voice to the wildly colored handkerchiefs he kept tied around his neck and the far-fetched stories he liked to tell. Uncle Reuben lived alone, halfway up the mountain at the Smith silver mine. Now and then, he joked about going into town and finding a woman to marry, but then he would let out a great big, rollicking laugh and ask, "But what woman would take me?"

Pa had three brothers who all lived somewhere in the canyon, but Uncle Reuben was the closest. Once a week or so, he would travel the ten miles down the mountain to eat Ma's cooking, restock his larder, and tell the Smith kids some tall tales.

As soon as dinner was over, the kids rushed to clear the table and clean the dishes. Ma smiled knowingly at Pa as they speedily did their chores without being asked. Then they pulled the chairs over to the fireplace and waited impatiently for Uncle Reuben to sit. The enormous fireplace sat in the middle of the ranch house against the wall that divided the living area from the bedroom where Ma and Pa slept. It provided warmth for both rooms, and it was where the family always gathered for games and stories or when Ma pulled down the old Bible to read to them before bed.

Uncle Reuben made a show of stretching, pulling his long arms behind his back. Then he walked to the water bucket to dip out a fresh mug. Sara squirmed with impatience but kept her mouth shut. Trying to hurry him along would just make him wink and go even slower, she knew. Finally, he pulled up one of the chairs right next to the hearth and settled in.

"Reckon I have a story to tell, if anyone wants to hear it," he drawled slowly.

"A true story or a made-up one?" demanded Levi.

"This one is true as the day I was born, happened only yesterday."

"Yesterday?" Tommy exclaimed. "Up at the mine?"

Uncle shook his head. "At my cabin, on the way home from work. You guys want to hear it?" There was a chorus of assent as everyone settled down in anticipation of the story—even Pa put down his almanac and pulled his chair closer to the fire.

"It was a gloomy day; the sun didn't peep through those thick clouds even once, and the rain was drizzly and cold. I left the mine early that day because it was so plumb miserable.

Then, as I was walking down the path to my cabin, I heard a noise in the woods to my left."

"What was it?" whispered Sara, leaning forward.

Levi shushed her. "Let him tell it, Sara!"

Uncle smiled. "I turned around, and nothing was there—nothing. I stopped to listen, and I couldn't hear anything. I couldn't hear anything at all!" He paused dramatically. "Not a bird chirp or a cricket song or even a rabbit scurrying through the weeds. The forest was dead silent."

The group around the fireplace was quiet, too, and the pop, crackle, pop of the fire sounded clearly in the room. Uncle Reuben took a deep breath, drawing out the moment.

"Now, I knew that something had to be scaring all the animals to make them be so quiet.

Scared me, too! I could feel the fear shivering up and down my spine. But still I couldn't see anything, so, slowly, I turned around and started walking back to the cabin. And then I heard it," he paused, the light from the flickering fire casting strange and dark shadows across his face, "footsteps behind me on the path."

"What was it?" Sara asked again, and this time no one shushed her. Everyone was leaning forward, waiting. Uncle Reuben smiled and took another drink.

"Well, I turned around, ever so slowly this time. Right there in the path, not ten feet away from me, was the biggest grizzly bear I'd ever seen! His fur was dark brown, almost black, and he was huge—meanest lookin' critter I've ever seen. He had an evil glint in his eye and a scar right across his snout. I looked at him, and he looked right back at me. We just stood there, and me so scared I couldn't move, my legs shaking like noodles, and my boots feeling like they was glued to the ground!"

"What did ya do?" Levi asked, bouncing on his knees. "Did you shoot him?"

"Nah, couldn't do it; my rifle was sitting on the table in my cabin. The very first thing I did was say a prayer. Yup, right there in the woods with my eyes wide open, I asked the Good Lord for a little bit of help. The bear didn't seem to like that none, though, because all of a sudden, he reared back on his hind legs and stood up tall. It seemed like he reached halfway to heaven himself; must have been ten feet tall!"

"Well, what happened then?" Sara demanded when Uncle Reuben stopped talking.

"Hang on there, girl; I need to wet my whistle."

He laughed and took another swig of his drink. Tommy jumped up and brought him a fresh mug full of water.

"Thankee, thankee, Tommy. Let's see, where was I? Oh yes, that bear was towering over me, blocking out all the daylight, and all of a sudden, he let out a massive bellow so loud I could feel it rattling my teeth as it rushed by. That's when my boots came unstuck from the ground, and they started running for the cabin all by themselves, pulling the rest of me with them. I knew that bear was chasing me because even over the pounding of my heart, I could hear his massive paws hitting the ground. Thu-thud, thu-thud, thu-THUD!"

Uncle Reuben suddenly stomped his feet down on the cabin floor, and everyone jumped in surprise. Ma dropped her knitting, and

Levi actually fell over, sprawling across Uncle Reuben's feet. Uncle Reuben threw his head back and laughed at the look on their faces, slapping his knees and sloshing his water everywhere. Levi wrapped his arms around Uncle Reuben's legs and waited for him to stop laughing.

"But what happened next?"

"Well, sir, I made it to the cabin first, and I've never been so happy to cross the threshold of that little shack. My whole goal was to get to my gun lying there on the table, but I never got the chance; the bear was right behind me, and I didn't even have time to close the door. The bear was shoving his way through the opening, and I knew that if he caught me, I was dead for sure. So I scampered up the ladder to the loft, quick as can be, and pulled the ladder up behind me."

"Did the bear go away then, when he couldn't

reach you?" Ma asked, quietly rocking in her chair while her knitting needles flashed in and out, in and out, through the pile of yarn back on her lap.

"Oh, he wasn't quite ready to give up yet, stubborn old beast like that," Uncle Reuben chuckled. "He spent some time pawing at the wall, trying to reach me, grunting and huffing up a storm to make his displeasure known. But that loft is twelve feet up, and no matter how he tried, he couldn't reach me. Then he decided to explore my cabin a little. He shredded my red quilt, the one that my mama made me, just tore it to pieces. Then he tried to climb on my table and broke it down to kindling, and my gun went flying across the room. It will probably never shoot straight again after that treatment," he said mournfully.

Sara giggled at the sad look on his face. "Then did he go away?"

"No, missy, he didn't! Not even then." He tousled Sara's curls and propped his feet up on the fireplace. "He wasn't done with me yet. Old Scar Face still had mischief to make. He started nosing in my cupboards, looking for food, I'm sure. But my larder was pretty empty, seeing as how it was Friday, and I was all set to come down to get some of your mama's sweet potato pie today.

"Finally, though, he managed to find something. In the very back of the cupboard was a rusty old bucket, and inside there was a bar of your ma's yellow lye soap. That old bear snuffled the bucket out, and when that bar of soap rolled out, he pounced on it like it was a fat ol' rabbit! He took a big bite right off the end of the bar and chewed down on it. Then he stopped and made the funniest face I ever did see; he looked confused and angry all rolled into one." Uncle Reuben screwed up his face into an expression of disgust, like he had a mouthful of crab apples, and growled at Tommy sitting next to him. The kids all laughed, and even Pa cracked a smile.

"But, it must not have tasted too good because suddenly he was growling and sneezing and spitting wildly. Chewed up soap was flying all over my cabin. And the noise he was making! He was yelping and growling and whining something fierce. But you can't get rid of the taste of soap that easy, you know, and he just got angrier and angrier, 'til suddenly, he reared back to his full height again. He took his claws, each one four inches long and sharp as a knife, and dragged them down my wall, tearing chunks out

of the logs, and across my cast-iron stove. And when he was done, there were ten grooves, clear as day, in the metal of my stove! And with that he lumbered out my door and back into the forest, still sneezing and spitting soap bits as he went."

Tommy's mouth was hanging open. "Did he really leave claw marks on your stove?"

"Ten clear tracks, my boy, one for each claw. I could put my whole first knuckle in the deepest one." Uncle Reuben held up his big hand to demonstrate how deep they were.

"Grizzlies are nothing to mess with," stated Pa. "There aren't many around anymore. He must be one of the last grizzly bears in California."

"Well, I hope after this he makes his way to Wyoming." Reuben banged down his empty mug on the hearth.

"You're blessed to be alive, Reuben. I hate to

think of you all alone in that awful old shack."
Ma shook her head. "You should move down
here with us."

"Well, I don't believe you," Levi proclaimed
loudly. "That was a made-up story, wasn't it?"

Uncle Reuben smiled. "You know, Levi, if
I hadn't seen the marks in my stove this very
morning when I woke up, I wouldn't believe me,
either. But the marks are there, my gun won't
shoot straight, and my ma's quilt had to go in the
rag bin, so it must have happened. But I kind of
thought you would need more proof, so go and
fetch my saddlebags for me."

Levi dashed out the door in an instant and
was back in seconds carrying the heavy leather
bags. Uncle Reuben's saddlebags were two large
leather pouches connected by a long strap. The
leather strap went over the back of the horse

so that one bag hung down on each side of the horse. Levi had the strap thrown over his shoulder so that one bag bounced against his stomach and the other smacked into his back while he walked.

"Let's see, let's see." Uncle Reuben took the bags and started digging in one. "Hmm, this can't be it." He pulled out a handful of small wrapped squares.

"Peanut brittle!" Sara squealed, spying the distinctive gold wrapping. "From Mr. Marshall's store! Oh, please, Uncle Reuben, can we have some?"

Ma was about to scold Sara for her manners, but Uncle Reuben just waved away her protest and handed out a piece to each of the kids and even slipped one to Ma and Pa. For several minutes the only sounds were the popping of the fire and the rustling of gold wrappers. While everyone was eating, Uncle Reuben searched in his bag for something else.

"Well, Levi, what do you think about this?" He pulled out a bar of yellow lye soap and held it flat on one big calloused palm for everyone to see. Or, more correctly, he held out half a bar of soap. Half was gone, and you could clearly see the teeth marks of the bear that had bit it off.

Levi's eyes went huge, and he goggled at the soap. "Wait! You mean that story was actually true?" he cried out.

"Every word, true as can be. You can all come up to the mine next week to see the marks yourself!" Uncle Reuben grabbed Levi up out of his chair and threw him over his shoulder with a loud bear roar. Tommy and Sara tried to run, but he grabbed each of them up with a strong arm and swung them around. The inside of the ranch house shook with love and fun and laughter, and rising above it all was Uncle Reuben's big booming laugh.

CHAPTER THREE

THE MYSTERY OF THE OPEN GATE

When the Smith kids came tramping down the mountain after their visit to the mine, they found a surprise waiting for them in the corral. Instead of their solid, scrubby work horses, there was a new stallion trying his paces in the enclosure.

"Oh!" Sara gasped in delight. "Isn't he beautiful?"

Truly he was, his coat sleek and shining in the sunlight. He was pure white from head to hoof, with no other markings. His silky mane and tail flowed halfway to the ground and bounced softly as he trotted. Even the way he moved was different, steady and strong, his muscles bunching and flexing beneath his smooth skin.

"Where did he come from?" Tommy asked with some awe as they pushed up to the fence of the corral. This was obviously an expensive horse, as different from their ranch horses as a rose is from a dandelion. Tommy hooked his arms over the top rail and watched the horse circle the small space.

"A beauty, ain't he?" Pa said, coming up behind them, holding the reins of old Duke, their piebald gelding. He pushed back his cowboy hat and swiped at his forehead with his sleeve.

"He surely is, Pa, but why is he here?" Levi asked in confusion. It was obvious that this was no ranch horse.

"A gentleman from the east is visiting California and was looking for a quiet place to board his horse while he spends a week at the sea. Someone in town recommended Crooked Creek. Old Sammy brought the horse out for him this morning. Wallerthon his name was, Mr. Isaac T. Wallerthon. How's that for fancy?" Pa grinned and ruffled Levi's hair. "You guys keep an eye on him while I work, OK?"

Pa swung up into Duke's saddle and headed off for the south pastures. Sara watched him go and then turned back to the corral.

"What do you suppose his name is?" she asked, climbing up on the first rail so she could see over the fence. The boys took up positions on either side of her.

"I think his name is Maximus," Tommy said stoutly.

"Nah," disagreed Levi. "He's all white; his name should have something to do with that. I would call him Cloud Jumper!"

Sara shook her head in disgust. "He's much too beautiful for those names. I think his name is Snowdrop."

Tommy looked at Levi, trying not to laugh. "Sara, he's a boy horse. You can't call a stallion Snowdrop!"

"Sure you can! Snowdrop, Snowdrop," she called out. The stallion stopped running and looked over at the kids. "See? He knows the name! Come here, Snowdrop."

The horse paced over to the kids, stopping a cautious five feet away and watching them. Sara cooed at him like he was a little baby.

"It's just a coincidence!" Tommy insisted.

Ma appeared in the doorway of the house,

"Oh, you kids are home! Come on in and have some lunch; tell me how your uncles are doing." She disappeared back into the house, and the kids jumped off the fence to follow her.

As they walked, Levi muttered to himself, "I ain't calling him Snowdrop, that's for sure."

At the dinner table that night, Tommy asked Pa what the horse's name was.

"His name?" Pa repeated, spearing a bite of chicken with his fork and dragging it through the brown gravy. "I don't rightly know; Old Sammy didn't say, if he even knew at all."

Old Sammy was a retired prospector who lived alone at the mouth of the canyon in a tiny one-room shack. He made money by helping all the ranchers with odd jobs and chores. Mr. Wallerthon had hired him to deliver his horse before heading to the ocean.

"So it might be Snowdrop, right, Pa?" Sara asked hopefully. Behind her Levi shook his head in disbelief.

"Snowdrop?" Pa grinned widely and started to respond when Ma caught his eye with a look. He hastily changed what he was about to say. "I guess it's possible, Sara-Bear, but I don't think it's likely."

Satisfied with that answer, Sara dug into her potatoes, and the conversation moved on.

Later that evening, Sara watched the beautiful horse from the single window in their loft bedroom. Pa had groomed him and fed him and locked him in the corral for the night. As she climbed into bed, she wondered if Pa would let her ride him tomorrow.

It felt like Sara had just closed her eyes when the rooster's crow split the morning air and the sun slanted through their bedroom window. Ma would be calling them soon to go feed the animals before breakfast. Sara grabbed the clothes she had stuffed into the bottom of the bed and quickly dressed under the covers. The clothes were toasty warm and made getting out of bed into the cold morning air less painful. Normally, Sara would skip down the steps as fast as possible to claim a spot in front of the fireplace, but today she paused at the window to look for the new horse. She pressed her nose against the cold, thick glass.

"He's gone! Tommy, Levi, he's gone!"

Tommy just grunted and then rolled over and pulled the blanket over his head, but Levi pushed up and looked at her in sleepy confusion.

"Who's gone?"

But Sara was already halfway down the stairs, yelling at the top of her lungs.

"Your Pa is already out looking for him," Ma told the anxious little girl, "and pray he finds him. I don't know what we'll do if we lose that horse; there's no way we could pay for him. The corral gate was wide open this morning," Ma said unhappily.

She shook her head as she used a fold of her skirt to open the door to the large cast-iron stove that took up most of one wall and shoved more wood in. "You'd best be gettin' on with your chores."

Tommy and Levi clattered down the stairs, still rubbing the sleep out of their eyes, and the three children went out the back door together. They all looked to the left automatically as they went out, watching the open corral gate swing in the slight breeze.

"How did he get out?" Tommy asked as he entered the barn and took the milking stool and pail over to Daisy Cow.

Levi slopped the pig and grabbed a shovel to clean out the stalls while he thought about it. "I reckon someone stole him. Horse like that'd be worth a lot of money."

"Don't be silly." Sara shook her head. She quickly gathered the eggs, avoiding Abner, their ornery rooster, who would peck you hard when you weren't watching. She reached for the eggs the old hen liked to hide behind the water dish. "Someone probably forgot to latch the gate." She carried the heavy basket of eggs toward the house, stopping to say good morning to each of the five work horses as she passed.

A piercing whistle stopped her in her tracks and had them all running to the stable door. Pa was coming 'round the house with the white horse in tow.

"You found him! Hurray!" shouted Levi, running toward Pa. The nervous horse whinnied and shied sideways at the noise, but Pa kept a firm hand on the bridle until he let him loose back in the corral.

"He was down in the south pasture. I must have forgotten to latch the gate last night." Pa shook his head and closed the gate behind the horse. A rope, tied in a loop with a small knot around the gate post, could be slipped over another post on the fence. Pa looped it twice for good measure. He slapped the fence and grunted, "There's no way he can get out of that!"

But he did. The next morning arrived with the gate wide open and the horse gone again. And the next, and the next. Every day for a week, Pa started his day by tracking down the missing horse, who was never far away. One morning they even found him in the barn, eating the spring hay. Every night Pa would make sure that the gate was tightly closed, but each morning it was wide open again. Who was opening the gate was a mystery much discussed at the dinner table.

"You think someone is playing a joke on us, Pa?" asked Tommy around a mouthful of stewed beans.

Ma shook her head. "Don't talk with your mouth full, Tommy. Who would do such a thing, anyway? There's no one close except the uncles, and they are all up at the mine this week."

"The gate is open each morning. Someone

has to be opening it." Pa frowned, his forehead wrinkling in worry.

"Well," Levi piped up suddenly, "I reckon that horse is jumpin' the fence and runnin away hisself!"

Pa started laughing. "He's a big horse, but even he can't jump that high; plus the gate would be closed if he was jumping it."

Levi blushed bright red. "Oh right, I forgot about that." He went back to shoveling the chicken and dumplings into his mouth. When no one was looking, he slipped his uneaten carrots to Flash under the table.

"Maybe it's some drifter passing through and having a laugh at us," Pa mused, scraping the last bit of food off his plate.

"At least whoever is doing it doesn't seem like they want to steal the horse, just cause some mischief. I'll be glad when Mr. Wallerthon comes tomorrow to pick up that horse. Nothing but trouble." Ma sighed as she pushed back from the table. "Anyone up for some buttermilk pie?"

While eating dessert, Tommy had an idea. "Say, what if Levi and Sara and I all slept in the stable tonight? We could keep watch over the horse and catch the person who keeps letting him out."

Ma frowned. "Absolutely not! What if it is a stranger who is doing it, and you three all outside? No, no, it won't do at all."

Pa nodded his agreement. "Your ma is right; it's not worth the risk, not even for that fancy horse. Get on up to bed now; that horse is leaving tomorrow one way or another."

The next day, after retrieving the horse from the meadow by the creek, Pa groomed the horse so that he was as beautiful and shiny as the day he came. Around noon Old Sammy came up the path, bringing Mr. Wallerthon himself to Crooked Creek. While not quite as fancy as his name, the man from the East still seemed rich and exotic to the Smith kids. He wore a pinstriped suit with a blue shirt and red tie. His shoes were pointed at the toe and shiny enough to see your reflection in them. He seemed a happy fellow, with a ready smile for everyone.

He was especially happy to see his horse, and the horse was equally excited to see his master. Mr. Wallerthon let out a piercing whistle, and the horse let out a loud whinny and raced across the corral to get to him. The man laughed and hugged the horse around his neck, patting his flank and then examining him closely.

"So, did my Barnaby give you any trouble?"

"Barnaby!" chorused all three children.

"Is that his name?" Sara exclaimed, terribly disappointed. "I thought it might be Snowdrop."

To Mr. Wallerthon's credit, he didn't even crack a smile. "That's a fine name, darling, but Barnaby he has been ever since the day he was born." Levi and Tommy assured him that it was a swell name for a horse, but Sara still looked doubtful.

"He was no trouble at all," Pa said, scratching his head nervously, "but we did have an issue you should know about." He went on to explain about the mystery of the open gate. "We never did figure out who was opening the gate every night."

To everyone's surprise Mr. Wallerthon let out a

knowing sort of chuckle. "Never fear, Mr. Smith. It was no fault of yours. I know exactly who was letting Barnaby out!"

"You do?" Pa asked, looking confused.

"I do. Let me show you something." With that he took Barnaby's bridle, walked him back into the corral, and closed the gate. Everyone followed him over to the corral fence.

"Barnaby," he addressed the stallion, who looked up alertly at his master as if he understood what he was saying. "Escape!"

At this command the horse immediately paced forward to the gate and carefully grasped the rope loop holding the gate closed in his front teeth. Then he backed up until the rope was tight and reared back on his hind hooves slightly. He came down and then repeated the action, hopping up and down over and over again.

Tommy looked at Pa in confusion; he'd never seen a horse act like this before. Pa's expression was puzzled at first, but then he noticed the rope loop slowly working its way up the post with every hop. Finally, it reached the top and popped off the post, the gate swung open, and the horse walked out. The whole escape took less than three minutes.

Mr. Wallerthon patted the horse and smiled at the shocked expressions on every face. "Barnaby is a circus horse, best trick pony this side of the Mississippi! Take a bow, Barnaby."

The horse crossed one front hoof over and bent forward in an unmistakable bow. The Smith kids burst out in applause.

"What else can he do?" Sara asked excitedly.

"Would you like a show," Mr. Wallerthon asked, "as a thank-you for putting up with my escape artist all week?"

The Smith kids all looked at Pa hopefully, who gave one of his mustache-twitching smiles. "All right, I guess chores can wait for a little bit. Run inside and get your ma; she'll want to see this. It's not every day we see a real live circus act at Crooked Creek Ranch!"

CHAPTER FOUR

FESTIVAL PREPARATIONS

The ranch house was filled with anticipation
and the intoxicating scent of pies, cookies,
breads, and cakes. Ma had spent the last two
days baking up a storm in preparation for the
Harvest Festival. Every year, after the harvest was
over but before the weather turned cold, all the
residents of the canyon came together for a big
celebration. This year it was the Smiths' turn to
host, and Ma had gone all out. The kitchen table
was groaning from the weight of all the baked
goods piled on top of it.

There were cookies in all shapes and sizes, from the beautifully browned molasses crisps, delicate and crumbly shortbread, and soft peanut butter cookies the size of your hand to Ma's specialty: snow-white sugar cookies cut into the shape of stars and moons. These were a rare treat in the Smith house because they were made from the expensive white flour that had to be purchased in town. Most of their treats were made from the heavier brown flour or cornmeal they ground themselves.

Alongside the cookies were sweet breads braided into wreaths and dotted with candied cherries or stuffed with raisins and nuts or rolled with cinnamon and brown sugar. Then came a small army of corn muffins and two beautiful apple pies with their pretty lattice tops. In pride of place in the center of the table, a beautiful

two-layer butterscotch cake was displayed, its surface covered in a thick layer of brown butter frosting. Ma had to keep a sharp eye out to prevent little fingers from sneaking a taste. The children could hardly contain their excitement. Tomorrow all of the neighbors would gather together, and there would be so much to do, to see, and, most importantly, to eat! Ma had even agreed that they could make root beer to drink at the festival. Tommy and Levi had only tasted that sweet, bubbly drink once before, and little Sara had never tasted it. It took two days to make the drink properly, so Ma said they would start this morning so it would be ready.

The children tried to hurry through their chore of stacking wood in the little shack by the back door. Stacking wood was a never-ending job for the family. The Smiths used fire to keep warm, to light the house, and for cooking, and it took an enormous amount of effort to keep that much wood ready to be used. A part of every day was given to replenishing the woodpile. Even Sara would help by carrying small armfuls of kindling from the woodpile to the house.

Once a month, the entire family would head into the woods. Pa and the uncles would locate dead trees and work together to fell them then the boys would use small axes to strip all the branches off the fallen trees. Ma and Sara would drag the branches away and load them into the wagon. Then Pa and the uncles would start the real work of breaking the trees down into manageable chunks with the two-handed saw. Tommy and Levi would roll the huge wooden wheels out of the way to where they would later be split into firewood. It was backbreaking labor but an absolute necessity for a family that had no other source of heat.

Once the woodpile was finally replenished, the kids ran inside, only to find mother taking off her apron and putting on her "going-to-town" hat.

"Where are you going, Ma?" Tommy asked in surprise.

Ma briskly tied the strings of her hat under her chin and picked up a basket off the table. "Mrs. Wilson is having her baby. Old Sammy just came to fetch me down to their homestead."

The children followed her out the front door to where the wagon was waiting. "Does that mean that Lizzie and John won't be coming to the festival?" Levi asked. John Wilson was the same age as Levi, and they hadn't seen each other since school let out in September to allow all the children to help with the harvest.

"We'll see how long it takes. If this baby comes quickly, I'll bring Lizzie and John back with me to the festival. That will give their mama some time alone with the new 'un." Ma handed Tommy the basket and gathered her skirts in one hand to climb up the wagon wheel and into the seat. Tommy passed the basket up to her.

"Now, children, I'll most likely not be back tonight, so I left a potpie on the stove. Make sure to finish your chores and keep your fingers out of the cake!" She gave Levi a hard stare, and he grinned a gap-toothed smile back at her.

"But, Mama," Sara asked, "what about the root beer? Who will make it if you're gone?" Her bottom lip started to quiver. "You promised I could try it."

Ma smiled down at the sad little girl. "I'm sorry, Sara-Bear, but Mrs. Wilson needs me. We'll make it another time." She took the reins in hand and clucked at Brownie and Pinto to get them moving. The three disappointed children sat down on the stoop and watched her drive down the lane until the wagon finally went around a bend and disappeared from sight.

"Well, that's that, I guess." Tommy sighed gloomily.

"What's what?" a cheerful voice asked from behind them. They all whipped around to see a slender man leaning against the corner of the house, cowboy hat in hand and a jaunty yellow bandana tied around his neck.

"Uncle Tom!" Sara squealed, standing up and launching herself at him. Dropping his hat, he caught her around the middle and hoisted her up onto his shoulders. She had to clutch at his hair when he started galloping around the yard.

Her wild giggles blended with the boys' laughter and Uncle Tom's deep chuckle. He carefully deposited Sara back onto the front stoop and sat down beside the boys.

"What's with the long faces?" he asked, pushing his lower lip out and making sad eyes at Sara.

"Ma had to go down to help Mrs. Wilson," Tommy explained, "so now we can't make root beer for the festival."

Uncle Tom looked down at the kids, blue eyes sparkling, and stroked his chin. "Who says you can't make root beer?"

"Ma is the only one who knows how to make it," Levi said grumpily. Then suddenly he looked up. "Wait! Do you know how to make root beer, Uncle Tom?"

"Do I know how to make root beer! Who do

you think taught your ma to make it? I taught her everything she knows!" He stood up and clapped his hands together. "Tom Jr., run over there and fetch my hat, and then I'll teach you all how to make the best root beer in California!" They all trooped back into the ranch house.

"Now," Uncle Tom started, pushing his sleeves up past his elbows, "we're going to need a big pot, the jug of molasses, a bucket of water from the well, plenty of firewood, your ma's yeast, sugar, and the root juice." The kids scattered to find all the ingredients while Uncle Tom stoked the fire in the stove, blowing on it to heat the coals to bright white and shoving in more firewood. Sara went to the shelves on the wall and came back with the jug of molasses and a canister of yeast while the boys ran out to bring in the other things.

When everything was assembled on the table, Uncle Tom directed Tommy to fill the large pot halfway up with sweet, cold well water. Then he turned the heavy brown jug of molasses over and let several cups of the sticky black-brown liquid ooze slowly into the pot. He carefully measured out a half cup of Ma's precious brown sugar. Using the big wooden spoon, he stirred it all together and then pushed the pot onto the stove where the heat was the hottest.

"Now what?" Sara asked, looking at the strange brown liquid doubtfully.

"The molasses syrup has to boil," he explained. "We need to keep the fire as hot as we can."

The kids gathered around the pot, waiting for it to boil, staring at the dark liquid.

"Don't you know a watched pot never boils?"

teased Uncle Tom. "Don't just stand there; we're going to need lots of wood to keep the fire hot. Go and fetch some extra kindling from the woodpile."

The kids ran to obey, and by the time they had restocked the woodpile, the molasses was boiling merrily on the stove. Uncle Tom used a towel to carefully pull the sticky mixture off the stove and placed it outside the back door to cool, covering it with a towel to keep the bugs out. "Now we need to wait about three hours for it to cool completely."

"Three hours?" Levi complained. "What are we supposed to do until then?"

"Have you finished your chores?" Uncle Tom asked.

All three children nodded promptly and watched him expectantly, hoping he would suggest a game, but Uncle Tom looked at them sharply. "What would you be doing if your mother were here?"

Levi groaned dramatically, his shoulders slumping forward. "Arithmetic and reading."

"Schoolwork at harvest time?" Uncle Tom asked, surprised.

Tommy grinned. "Teacher told Ma that Levi was behind in his work, so she makes him do his times tables and read a page in his primer every afternoon. I've got to dig a fire pit for the feast."

Uncle Tom clapped Levi on the shoulder in sympathy. "Sorry, boy-o, it's schoolwork for you; hop to it. Tommy, I'll help you with that fire pit. And what about you, little miss; what's your assignment?"

"Ma wants me to air out all the winter quilts for the company."

"All right, then; we all have our marching orders. Let's get to work." He gave Sara a quick salute and then turned around and started marching in place. "Hup, two, three, four, hup, two, three, four!" And with that he marched Tommy right out the door, heading for the tool shed. Sara hummed to herself as she pulled all the colorful quilts out of the large chest. They had an odd, musty smell from the mothballs that were packed in with them. One by one, Sara hung the quilts up over the fence to air out and freshen in the sunshine. As she trooped in and out of the house with each one, she could hear Levi muttering to himself.

"Two times two is four; two times three is six; two times four is eight . . ."

The time passed quickly as they prepared for the festival. Levi finished his work and went out to help dig the pit with Tommy and Uncle Tom. At noon they stopped for a luncheon of corn bread, apples, and walnuts, eaten right there on the floor in front of the fireplace. Sara watched in fascination as Uncle Tom ate his entire apple, core, seeds, and all, in five big bites. He winked at her. "Waste not, want not!"

Finally, the molasses was deemed suitably cool, and they all gathered around the big pot again. Uncle Tom carefully unscrewed a jar full of murky brown liquid, labeled "Root Extract" in Ma's best handwriting. Sara pressed forward to see the amazing juice that turned molasses into root beer and took a big sniff.

"Oh! That smells terrible!" Wrinkling her nose, she hastily backed away from the jar, covering her nose with her sleeve. "What is in that?"

"It is a little pungent, isn't it?" Tom agreed,

rubbing his nose briskly. "It changes each time, but I think this one has burdock root, cherry tree bark, and sassafras root." He carefully poured the smelly liquid into the molasses syrup mixture and mixed it together.

"Will it taste good?" Sara asked doubtfully.

"Don't worry, little bear, it will be delicious! Now, I like my root beer really foamy, and this is what we need." He pulled a canister over to him. "Two spoonfuls of yeast to give our root beer its fizz." He carefully measured off two spoonfuls of yeast and dumped them in. Then with a wink at Sara, he dumped another pinch in. "For extra fizz!" After mixing everything together, Uncle Tom set the pot aside and covered it with a towel.

"All right, kiddos, it's got to rise until nighttime. Then we'll strain it with some cheesecloth, and before bed tonight we'll get it all bottled up.

Now, you kids hop to your afternoon work, and I am going to head out and help your Pa with the stock. We'll be back in time for dinner." He grabbed his hat off the hook and disappeared out the back door.

The boys followed him out the door, planning to go check their trap line. Pa paid them one penny for every five gophers they caught.

Gophers were a huge problem for every rancher in the canyon. A single gopher could burrow beneath your garden and eat out all the roots of your vegetables before you even knew he was there. In the pastures their tunnels could cave in underneath the cows' hooves, sometimes breaking the leg of the unfortunate animal.

Sara knew it was time for her to sweep the ranch house, but as she pulled out the whisk broom made from cornstalk branches, she kept eyeing the bowl of root beer in curiosity. Tommy and Levi had been telling her about the fizzy drink for years. They loved to tell her all about how it foamed when you opened it and how it bubbled in your mouth, unlike any other drink. She had waited so long to try it.

Uncle Tom had left the canister of yeast on the counter next to the bowl. If two spoonfuls of yeast made it nice and fizzy, would four spoonfuls make it super fizzy? She crept over to the counter and looked under the towel at the strange brown liquid. The yeast in there had already started to foam up on the surface. A little more yeast couldn't hurt, right?

Suddenly making up her mind, she quickly dumped in two more scoops and re-covered the pot. Wouldn't the boys be surprised when they tasted the fizziest root beer that ever there was?

Smiling in anticipation, she started sweeping the floor with all her energy. Everything needed to be clean for the festival tomorrow.

Chapter Five

Root Beer Catastrophe

The day of the Harvest Festival dawned clear, with not a cloud in the sky. All three Smith children were up before the rooster even started crowing his morning song. Who could sleep on Festival day? There were cookies on the table, chairs set up in the meadow, and a beautiful jug of root beer chilling in the creek.

The night before, Uncle Tom had shown them how to strain the root beer by slowly pouring it through a thin piece of cloth. Then he had carefully poured it into Ma's largest jug and sealed the small opening tight and wedged it into the shallow part of the creek behind the house with several large rocks to prevent it from floating away.

The children hurried through their morning chores more cheerfully than usual. Sara was in such a hurry that she forgot to say good morning to the horses and ended up stepping on one of the eggs she was supposed to be collecting. Even the animals seemed to sense it was a special day—the normally placid horses were restless and frisky in their stalls while Levi measured out their grain, and old Daisy kicked over the pail twice before finally letting down her milk for Tommy. Flash ran in circles around the children, barking and constantly getting underfoot until Tommy ordered him out of the barn.

After chores there was only time to cram a

piece of corn bread in their mouths when they heard a shout from the front of the house.

"Hello! Hello! We're here!"

The first of the wagons started rolling up the hill. The Jensens were the closest family down the canyon, their five children hanging off every part of the wagon and waving frantically as they pulled in. Pa directed them to leave their wagon on the edge of the meadow where the bonfire would be. Just minutes behind them, the Simmonses and the Walkers rode in. As soon as they arrived, the families started unpacking their wagons, carrying their food offerings to the tables by the fire pit. Pots of baked beans and potato salad, Mrs. Walker's famous sauerkraut, bags of new apples and carrots, bowls of hard-boiled eggs, and pans of corn bread and soda biscuits all adorned the tables.

Wagon after wagon rolled up the hill to the meadow until there were fourteen wagons in a semicircle around the edge of the meadow. Everyone in the canyon was there except for the Wilsons and, of course, Ma, who was down helping Mrs. Wilson have her baby. Levi jumped up and raced to the hill every time a wagon pulled in to see if it was Ma bringing Lizzie and John Wilson to the festival, but they never appeared.

After the food was unloaded, each family made up their beds for the night so no one would have to leave the party early. Stout wool blankets and colorful quilts with dazzling patterns were laid out in wagon beds, underneath the wagons, and wherever a flat space could be found. Once this chore was done, the kids were finally released to go play, and there was a stampede of children out of the meadow and down to the pasture by the creek.

There were children of all ages, from Seth Foster, who at fifteen wasn't quite ready to leave the kid games and go work with the men, to little Delia Walker, who at three was finally old enough to leave her mama's apron and toddle after her older sisters. The girls immediately divided into two groups and started a game of skip rope, two girls in the middle with skirts flying and braids bouncing as they jumped over the long rope swung by two other girls, one on each end. All the girls sang a skipping song to help them keep their rhythm:

"Apples, peaches, pears, and plums
Tell me when your birthday comes!
January, February, March, April . . ."

The boys ran past the girls, heading straight

for the creek, where they skipped rocks, made small boats out of bark and leaves, or rolled up their pants to wade in and look for frogs. The surprised yelps of those dipping their feet into the cold water echoed up the canyon and back again.

The mothers watched the kids run off and then gathered at the table where they could keep an eye on the playing children and tend to babies and food at the same time. They chatted easily with one another as they worked on arranging everything for the midday meal. They exchanged recipes and quilting patterns and shared funny stories of the trouble their children had caused during the break from school.

For the men, however, it wasn't time to rest or play. It was customary for the men to spend the morning helping the host family with some special project on their farm. Sometimes they would have a barn raising, help slaughter the spring pigs, or cut wood for the winter. Working together, the men could accomplish in one day what would take the family months to do. It was a way of saying thank you for hosting the festival, and, more importantly, a way of giving back to the community. In such an isolated section of the California wilderness, it was important to be on good terms with and help care for your neighbors.

Pa had thought long and hard about what the men would do and had finally decided to clear an additional five acres of field on the north pasture. He would plant extra hay in the spring, not only to feed the stock, but to sell in town and earn some extra money. The men, carrying axes and large two-handled saws over their shoulders, started off to the north. Soon, all could hear the rhythmic *chop, chop* of the axes, and occasionally the ground would shake with the fall of a mighty oak tree.

The morning passed quickly and happily as everyone renewed friendships and enjoyed their rare day of relaxation. At noon everyone paused for a simple lunch, sitting wherever there was room on blankets, wagons, chairs, and logs rolled up from the woodpile. The men, red and sweaty from a solid morning's work, rejoined the group and stretched out on the ground to rest.

"Can we have the root beer now?" Sara tugged on Uncle Tom's sleeve as he lay under the sycamore tree, resting. He tipped his hat back off his face and smiled up at the excited little girl.

"No, sweetie, that's for the feast tonight." He

smiled at her crestfallen expression and handed
her a shiny red apple.

Disappointed, Sara went over to a log, rested
her chin in her hands, and took a big bite of
the apple. After chewing a couple of times, she
stopped suddenly, cocking her head to the side to
listen closely.

Mary Jane Clark, sitting next to her on the log,
looked up when Sara stopped eating. "What's
wrong, Sara?"

"I think I hear—" Sara closed her eyes and
listened harder, trying to hear over the chatter
and laughter of the kids around her. "Yes! I
hear a wagon!" In her excitement the apple was
dropped in the dirt and forgotten as she jumped
up and ran for the road.

Coming around the bend at that very moment
was Ma in the wagon. Sara waved with all her

might, and then she saw not one, but three people waving back.

"Levi, Ma is back, and she's brought John and Lizzie!"

Levi let out a joyous shout and ran to join Sara. By the time the wagon and Ma made it to the top of the hill, all of the kids and most of the adults had joined the welcoming committee. Ma laughed and passed John and Lizzie down to waiting hands.

"The Wilsons have a fine baby girl! Eight pounds and a great set of lungs. You could have heard her howling a mile away." Everyone cheered—a birth at harvest time was a happy thing. The women surrounded Ma and pulled her to the table to tell them all about the birth, so she left the reins of the horses in Tommy's hands. Levi and Tommy hurried to strip the tack off Brownie and Pinto, curry them, and bed them down in their stalls, John Wilson tagging along and chattering nonstop about the birth of his newest sister.

"Let's play hide-and-seek!" Lizzie Wilson called out. There was a general murmur of agreement, and soon the children were scattering in every direction, looking for a hiding spot while Lizzie counted to one hundred behind one of the wagons.

The adults took advantage of the free time to play games, too. Families pulled out handmade chess and checkerboards and decks of cards.

Pa came out of the house carrying his cribbage board. Cribbage was a popular game in the canyon, and nearly every family had their own board. It was a thin round of wood cut from a sycamore tree and carefully sanded and polished until it was as smooth as butter. Then it had been stained with walnut husks until it was a deep burnished brown color. Pa had carefully used a nail and hammer to make two rows of holes around the entire edge of the board, and he had carved by hand four tiny wooden pegs to fit into the little holes. In the evenings Pa sometimes took out the board and spent an hour or two studiously carving designs into the center of the board.

"Who's first?" Pa demanded, dealing two piles of six cards. He smiled when Ma claimed the seat across from him and picked up one of the piles. Sara, who never liked to play hide-and-seek, snuggled up to Ma's side to watch. She was still too young to play, but she loved to watch the little pegs move around the board.

After losing two games, Pa threw his cards

down with a laugh. "I give up! Anyway, it's time to light the bonfire." He pushed back from the table, and his place was quickly claimed by Mrs. Walker. Pa lit the wood already piled in the fire pit and blew on the small flame to encourage it. Once the fire was burning well, he slowly added sticks of red oak to it. They needed a good coal base for the barbecue, and Pa had a fresh haunch of beef to cook on the spit.

The lighting of the fire signaled a change in the activities. The games came to a stop, and the contests began. The boys and girls had races, running around the house, down to the creek, and back again. They had three-legged races with two children tied together and finally sack races, hopping down the length of the meadow in coarse flour sacks. The moms and dads cheered on their racers and groaned or laughed as the children fell over or ran into each other. Little Delia Walker tried her very first three-legged race with her sister but couldn't figure out the stride, so the pair kept turning in circles and never got anywhere close to the finish line.

By then the fire had burned down to a lovely white-red coal bed, and Pa and some of the other men carefully spitted the beef and lowered it over the fire. Soon the smell of the meat permeated the entire meadow.

"Is it time for the root beer now?" Sara asked Uncle Tom.

"Soon, Sara-Bear, very soon!" Uncle Tom picked her up and set her on his shoulders. "Why don't you come with me and watch me beat Uncle Reuben in the shooting contest?"

Shooting targets were set up at the bottom of

the hill at distances of fifty, one hundred, and two hundred yards. Uncle Tom and Sara joined the crowd heading in that direction. There were as many women as men in this contest and a good number of the boys as well. Judy Simmons was one of the best shots in the county at close range and regularly hit the bullseye at fifty yards with her rifle. And despite Uncle Tom's boast, Reuben Smith easily won the two-hundred-yard challenge.

Next, the men lined up for a log-splitting contest to see who could split the most logs in five minutes. The axes swung up and down, their silver heads flashing in the afternoon sunshine, and the steady *thwack, thwack* of splitting logs filled the air, along with the cheers of encouragement from the audience. Mr. Simmons set a new record of forty-eight on his first try and looked like the winner until Mr. Foster, his face almost purple from exertion and puffing like a steam engine, managed forty-nine at the last second. The men all clapped and cheered.

"Time for dinner!"

The call rang out over the meadow, and everywhere the kids abandoned what they were doing and swarmed back to the fire pit. Dishes were being uncovered on the table, and everyone grabbed a plate and started to line up by the fire pit, where Pa was armed with a carving knife.

Sara ignored the line waiting for food and ran through the crowd looking for Uncle Tom. She found him standing by the fire with Pa. He smiled when he saw her coming.

"Is it time for root beer now?" she demanded, swinging on his arm.

"Yes!" Uncle Tom declared. "It's time for root

beer. I already sent Tommy down to the creek to grab it. Look! There he is."

Tommy was trudging across the meadow with the heavy root beer jug slung across his shoulders, dripping water all down his shirt from its dunking in the creek. Uncle Tom took the jug from him and looked around. The table was crowded with dishes, food, and people eating. There was no room there to open and serve the root beer.

"Let's take it over to the Rock," he decided. The three of them headed for the edge of the meadow where a large outcropping of sandstone jutted out of the ground. The top of the Rock was relatively flat and made a good place to set up.

"Levi! John! We're going to open the root beer now!" Tommy yelled out. Everywhere blonde, brown, and black heads popped up from their dinner plates.

"Root beer!"

Soon all the kids were trailing behind Uncle Tom as he carried the rare treat, each carrying his or her own little cup to receive a small portion of the beverage. Uncle Tom set the jug down on the Rock and took out his pocketknife. The jug had a small mouth with a tight cork plugging the hole, and Uncle Tom had covered the whole thing with a layer of wax to protect it from leaking in the creek. He carefully used his knife to cut away the wax covering.

While the kids waited anxiously and poor little Sara was practically shaking with excitement, Uncle Tom cleaned his knife and put it away.

"All right, I'm going to pull the cork out now. Be careful; a little of the root beer might spill out once the cork is out."

The kids backed away a foot or so but then

eagerly pressed forward again as Uncle Tom grabbed the cork and started to pull.

Nothing happened. Uncle Tom frowned and took a tighter hold on the cork and pulled again. His face wrinkled up in concentration as he slowly wiggled the cork left and right in the opening. Slowly it started to come free.

"Ah-ha!" Uncle Tom exclaimed, as he finally pulled the cork free from the jug. He held the jug up in triumph.

And then it exploded!

Root beer shot out of that jug, rising a full twenty feet into the air and shooting in every direction. Uncle Tom was wrestling with the suddenly slick jug as it tried to shoot out of his hands! For a second all of the kids watched the fountain shooting up in the sky with their mouths hanging open in amazement. Then all

that root beer started coming down, soaking everyone within a ten-foot radius. Sticky brown liquid landed on their heads and dripped down their faces, off their noses, and down their backs. Poor Sara was the closest, and there was not a spot on her body that was not completely drenched in the longed-for root beer. Within seconds all of the root beer had shot out of the jug.

There was a moment of complete silence as the children looked at each other, straggly wet hair dripping root beer into their stunned eyes, and back at Uncle Tom, who had managed to miss most of the downpour as he grappled with the squirming jug. Then the laughing started back at the firepit, where most of the adults had been safe from the deluge but had a great view of the entire catastrophe. The roar of the laughter increased when the children turned to look at their parents. Uncle Reuben was laughing so hard he had to cling to the back of a wagon to stay upright. The mothers, still laughing heartily, headed toward the pathetic and sodden group to help clean up.

Sara, always the one to recover first, shook back the wet hair out of her face and licked some of the sticky sweet juice off her arm. She smiled brightly up at Uncle Tom as root beer ran down her face and dripped off the tip of her nose.

"It is delicious!"

Later that evening, after all the sticky children took a shivery cold bath in the creek, after all the food was devoured and only crumbs remained, and after the singing and the dancing were done, Ma tucked three exhausted children into bed. She pulled off Levi's boots one by one as he fell into the bed, already half asleep. She lovingly pulled the quilt up to Tommy's chin and smoothed back his hair. He smiled sleepily, rolled himself into a little ball, and closed his eyes. Ma moved to Sara's side of the bed and dropped a kiss on her forehead. To her surprise tears started to well up in Sara's eyes, spilling over and rolling down her cheeks.

"Why, Sara-Bear! What's wrong? Didn't you have fun at the festival?"

Sara sniffled, rubbing her nose with an arm that still smelled faintly of root beer. "Yes! It was the best festival ever, but now it's over, and it won't come back for a whole year!" She pulled the quilt over her face as she began to cry in earnest.

Ma smiled. "It's true, the Harvest Festival is

over, but every day brings us new blessings, and guess what." Ma gently stroked the top of Sara's head. "Soon it will be Christmas."

"Christmas!" Sara pulled down the quilt and smiled up at her mother, dimples appearing in her tear-stained cheeks. "Really?"

"Really, really," Ma promised. "Now go to sleep, little one." Sara closed her eyes obediently and was sound asleep and dreaming of Christmas before Ma even reached the stairs.

Check out these other Level 3 books from
The Good and the Beautiful Library.

Mr. Apple's Family
By Jean McDevitt

The Journey of Ching Lai
By Eleanor Frances Lattimore

New Boy in School
By May Justus

David and the Seagulls
By Marion Downer